YOU DON'T
GET TO THE OCEAN
BY ACCIDENT

YOU DON'T GET TO THE OCEAN BY ACCIDENT

Discover the Power of Your Story
and Decide How to Harness It

BRANNAN SIRRATT

Contact me at *brannansirratt.com*.

Cover and interior layout by Cindy Curtis

ISBN 979-8-9879466-0-2 (paperback)
ISBN 979-8-9879466-1-9 (ebook)

First Edition: March 2023

This paperback edition first published in 2023

For everyone with an idea who isn't sure if that makes them an author. It does, but that doesn't matter right now.

It's your story (and the you that it came from) that I'm wildly interested in.

I hope one day soon you'll see what I see.

CONTENTS

INTRODUCTION

LET'S JUST GET OUR FEET WET

This is the part where I tell you who I am. Anyone who's written about themselves (or avoided doing so) knows that's easier said than done. For years, my Instagram profile read "accidental editor." On Twitter, it was, "I didn't mean to become an editor." My personal account may still say that, in fact—and unless something magical happens from the time I am typing this to the time I save and share, Twitter will too. Careful not to get dust in your eyes when you swipe over to check.

I know now that this is not true. I still think it's quippy and funny for any context other than a professional connection. (Sorry, Twitter. Someday, if you get your act together.) In any case, when I first typed those words, I genuinely meant them. I used them in my consult calls and built them into my bios and "the story" of my background. *Build* is probably too strong a word. It was simply what came out of me when pressed. Take a moment there: when pressed to convey my credentials, the juiciest story I could access was that life simply happened to me and I went with it.

"I CHOSE NOTHING. I WAS BORN, AND THIS IS WHAT I AM."

—BRAD PITT'S ACHILLES

Brad Pitt made it sound way cooler. In the movie *Troy*, he does a lot of jaw clenching, nostril flaring musing about fate and legacy. I know this because my husband has very different comfort shows than I do, and Troy is one of them. (I keep Scrubs, Schitt's Creek, Parks and Rec, and the Office queued up. He has this and a specific scene from Peaky Blinders. We'll both fall back to New Girl. I digress.)

Two quotes from Troy have set up permanent residence in the corner of my mind. One is from a scene with Briseis. Achilles tells her, "You must be royalty. You've spent years talking down to men." That one has much more to do with religious trauma and being a precocious #audhd child than anything that matters here. But the first one—*I chose nothing. I was born, and this is what I am*—comes up a lot.

Funny thing is, I am a huge proponent of agency and choice. A good bit of my encouragement to clients is that they get to decide what done looks like, what they want to create, how they want to create it. I never subscribed to arguments against free will, and I have a side-eye relationship to anything fate-centric.

And yet, I *really* resonated with this quote. Something about releasing responsibility for my circumstances appealed to me, and I supposed it would for that version of Achilles, too. The warrior who's about to face everyone he's killed *would* want to believe he had no say in the matter. But there he was, choosing that same circumstance over and over again. It's a gorgeous line. It's utter bullshit. And I bought in, completely—until I didn't.

This is a long way of saying that I chose everything. I was born, and there were a thousand versions of me that could have emerged from there, but they didn't. Or they haven't yet, anyway. Some things were always going to be, but they weren't the parts that mattered. Not really. All of those parts have been forged from choice and failure and success and more choice. The best part about it all for me is that my choices have led me to dozens of incredible people choosing to emerge as authors for the first time in the life they were born into. They are experts and teachers and warriors and nurturers, who made hard choice after hard choice inside of circumstances both chosen and not. And in that space of emerging, each has a story that has a thousand "right" versions—a how-to and a memoir and a novel and a podcast and a quiet whisper to a friend. Our job is to discover the one that feels best now. The one that says, "this is what I am." The one we want to choose.

No one gets to that space by accident, just like you wouldn't stumble up to the ocean. I have to drive a long way east or west (sometimes south, in a pinch) to hit sand, and when I do, it's because I've arranged my whole life to allow for it. Even folks who live in a coastal town make preparations to spend time on the beach—and not all beach days are the same. There are times and places to swim, snorkel, walk, read, play games in the sand, and hunt for shells and clams. I'm painting with broad brushes here, because anyone who's taken that rearranged-life-trip with me knows that I will pull over anywhere that I see surf, go plop myself into the sand, and not move for hours. Sunblock, snacks, and towels be damned. *And even then*, I'm not surprised when I see it. I'm looking for it. I'm choosing it.

Here's where the first of many metaphors, analogies, and similes (I never could name those right) comes together: we are all oceans. You and your book, me and mine, and us and our work together. And an ocean is a whole lot of power that most of us have to rearrange our lives to acknowledge.

Where I've gotten hung up, and where I see many of my clients and peers getting hung up, is not in seeing the power of story. We know what it is to have a book and be an author, even in small ways like a booklet or a blog. And that's exactly what makes us shy away. Some other identity outside of *author* takes precedent—an ocean we already know how to visit without getting caught in a current or overtaken by the tide. If we're even going to consider writing a book, we have to do it side-eyed, not quite able to look directly at the truth that author is us and we are author.

But at the point where you have enough of your thoughts in hand that a book comes into consideration, you've already made choices. You've rearranged your life time and time again. You've started off in a direction and didn't look back. You've had times of immersion and times of stillness and times of rest.

It might feel safer sometimes to consign ourselves to literary fate, especially when we don't feel called to be writers, or if that calling feels so brand new it might shatter if we look at it too closely. So we might play with an idea forever and hope the muse swoops in to finish it for us. We might keep it close to the chest, only working on it when no one is looking for fear they might see it and make it too real to ignore. Or we might talk about it everywhere, hoping the conversation alone makes it real enough to ignore the work.

That's where the best part of my job *for you* comes in: you didn't get here by accident, but I know these currents. Pull over to this inlet for a bit. I won't let you drown. Sit with me, and let's just take in the power of this story, this teaching, this wisdom that all the choices of your life have brought you to. Let's get our feet wet. Maybe get a little messy. And see what we might discover.

ETHOS

WHAT'S IN YOU IS WORTH TELLING

People are sometimes surprised to find that I'm not a "red pen editor." I think it's old school-year wounds, where we're not quite sure how we feel about something until there's a grade on it...or maybe that's just me. In any case, developmental editing is very different from proofreading, which I've done plenty of as well. Proofing is based on objective standards (though the objectives can change based on your preferred style's school of thought) and is about finding all the wrong things in the words you've strung together. Developmental editing is about finding the strings of words that feel right altogether.

There are a thousand different versions of your book that *could* exist in the world as objectively good. There is the novel version, the business how-to version, the memoir. There is a graphic novel and a poetry collection and an academic exploration. There is something all about you and something that keeps you in the background. That's the good news and the terrible news all rolled up into one: you have *all* of the options, which means you have all of the options. And I can't tell you which one to choose.

"YOU ALREADY KNOW WHAT YOU'RE GOING TO DO. EVERYBODY DOES."

—FIONA SHAW (AUNT PETUNIA) AS A THERAPIST IN FLEABAG

I can't tell you when you're done. I can't tell you if you're on the right track. What I can tell is when you feel like you're on the right track. I've got enough pattern-tracking hours under my belt that I can spot the red flags and the hesitance. I can see your eyes light up and your body lean in. I can see it flowing on the page and I can see when it's stuck behind the lump in your throat that says "This matters, and here's why I'm scared to let the world know it does." And when I can't tell, I can ask.

In *Fleabag*, a running theme of season 2 is that Fleabag keeps saying she doesn't know what to do and wants someone else to tell her—but the characters around her keep reminding her that she knows exactly what she wants. I think you do, too. Our work isn't for me to tell you what to say or how. It's to help you see—and unlock and own—what you already know. Even if you don't know it yet. It's in you. Writing is one way to get it out.

TO THE OCEAN!
HOW TO USE THIS WORKBOOK

This is a reformatting and reimagining of the discovery series I work clients through, usually when they're at a turning point in their writing process. Maybe it's going from ideation to actually writing, or sorting out a collection of posts and transcripts, or revising a manuscript. Sometimes, we know what we need and get right to that tool—a refreshed table of *content* (no, that's not a typo), a refined analysis arc...But not often.

In most cases, we start with what I've called a "discovery" call regardless of how much has already been discovered. It never hurts to go back and refine who you are to your work, who your reader is, and how the work brings you together. That one step can solve so much more than we realize.

With that said, you may decide one step looks more advantageous than another, based on where you are with your idea or project, and you're welcome to skip right to it. I will always recommend going top to bottom, though, just in case you find an answer to a question you didn't know you had.

Because this is a book and not a 1:1 call, I've tried to lay it out with as much context as I could manage, while keeping the bulk of the page time free for you to explore. After all, our goal here is for you to do the discovering. So I've grouped each step into three parts that form a tool all on their own:

- Find Access Points
- Make Connections
- See What Comes Up

When you're starting a new project or feeling stuck in something old: look for ways you can easily tap into what you want to write (find access points) and set the blocked up stuff aside for now; set some guidelines using reference points—authors you love, a specific target reader, and your relationship to your topic (make connections); then start drafting, even if that looks like making lists, without judging (see what comes up).

Inside of these sections, there are short explanations preceding a series of questions and writing prompts. There's not much space to write here, and that's also by design. I do want you to take the time to contemplate each question, but sometimes more words indicates less understanding. There's a balance to strike between free writing and writing around a topic. Have we found it with these pages? Who knows. I recommend writing in pencil and grabbing extra erasers.

You're also more than welcome to type, to make up your own questions, to get 2 pages in and realize the lightbulb is on and your whole book is coming to you like you've trapped a Muse in the attic (this is a *Sandman* reference; please don't be that guy). My point is, this is yours now. I hope something in it will inspire you and reignite your passion to write. If not, that's okay too. Put it on the shelf for a better "beach day," or hand it off to a friend who's been dying to catch a glimpse of their own shoreline. And as always, just like a buffet before COVID-times, please take what you like and leave the rest.

FIND ACCESS POINTS

REFRAME YOUR
RELATIONSHIP TO THE
PROCESS OF WRITING
AND THE PROJECT
YOU'RE EXPLORING

THE PROCESS

WHEN WE CAN'T SHOW UP WRONG, WE START TO SHOW UP FULLY

Everyone's relationship to writing is a little bit different. We like to joke in memes and writing groups about how painful it can be—but humans are messy, and we don't get to rely on universal standards to tell us about our experience. As the infamous "they" say: *What got you here won't get you there*. What worked last time may be awful this time. Writing isn't all bad or all good, and one tool isn't wholly useful or totally trash. Absolutes are the realm of "should," and should has no jurisdiction here.

So our first order of business is to go for the Bs: it's time to bitch and brag. Lay it all on the table. What has you stuck enough to start stringing Google terms together to find an editor, or to ask your friend how they finished their book, or to collect a thousand and one process books and social media accounts and any tool or process you can find that'll help you get. this. book.

done already? Which of those books and processes did you *hate*? Which did you love?

EVERYONE'S RELATIONSHIP TO WRITING IS DIFFERENT. "SHOULD" HAS NO JURISDICTION HERE.

Or maybe you're not feeling stuck at all. What was that point that made you feel like you were done (in a good way), and what was your experience of writing to that point? What strengths are you bringing to the table? We're edging into *brag* territory here, but the counterintuitive encouragement I have for you is to brag whether or not it's done or feels good or meets some absolute standard. Whether you "should" brag means nothing at all. That's just another false absolute.

What has kept you at the table, day after day, writing or thinking about your topic or toying with the shapes it might take in the world? What tools and methods do you absolutely love and swear by no matter what else might come your way? What does flow look like for you, and how can we make that our objective all the time? I want to know it *all*. Because it's all important, because it's all you and because you cannot show up "wrong." You can only show up. When you believe you can't show up wrong, you show up fully. And that's where magic happens.

Where are you in the book-writing process? Do you have a publishing vision (traditional, self-pub, hybrid, something else)?

_____

_____

_____

_____

_____

_____

_____

What obstacles have you faced so far, and what kind of support would you like for those things?

_____

_____

_____

_____

_____

_____

_____

_____

What do you love most about writing, books or otherwise? What does "flow" look like for you?

_____

_____

_____

_____

_____

_____

_____

_____

_____

_____

What frustrates you most about writing, books or otherwise? What does "blocked" look like for you?

_____

_____

_____

_____

_____

_____

_____

_____

_____

_____

What are you looking for in a writing partner, support group, book coach, or editor?

_____

_____

_____

_____

_____

_____

_____

_____

_____

Think of your best writing experiences and your worst writing experiences—what does past-you want current-you to know about those situations or project types?

_____

_____

_____

_____

_____

_____

_____

_____

_____

NOTES:

_____

_____

_____

_____

_____

_____

_____

_____

_____

_____

_____

_____

_____

_____

_____

_____

_____

_____

_____

_____

_____

_____

THE PROJECT

NO ONE IS FORCING YOU TO WRITE—SO WHAT IS IT THAT'S KEEPING YOU HERE?

This is the first question I ask on a consult call: why a book? I know I can get a ton of conversation and detail out if I ask about your topic. If there's one thing writers aren't good at, it's concisely explaining what they're writing about. (We'll get to that later, though, because I want *you* to be good at that.) But I don't really care about that just yet. Not because I'm not interested in your topic, but because we both already know that there's interest in your topic. You've talked to friends about it, taught clients about it, worked colleagues through it. You've seen specials and read books and listened to podcasts.

What we don't yet know is why you're drawn to put that specific topic into book form. Honestly, most of the forms mentioned in the last paragraph are a lot easier to access than writing a whole-ass book. And they're just as viable for reaching a wide range of audiences. So what is it about a book that has you here, doing this work?

WE SOMETIMES WANT TO *HAVE WRITTEN* A BESTSELLING BOOK, NOT TO WRITE AND SELL A BOOK.

Sometimes, I wonder if the meme "Writers don't want to write; they want to have written" is as true for nonfiction as it is for fiction. Because more often, I see us enjoying the process of expressing ourselves on the page but pulling back when it's time to consider that page being read by anyone. You may relate to one of these two examples:

One: *I want to write a bestseller and get picked up by The Daily Show and get on a TED main stage. But when I try to picture the TED topic or who I'd have to hand the book to in order to get on the show or where I would promote the book, the vision gets blurry.* **Two:** *I know exactly what I want to say and why, and honestly I just want to impact one person, somehow. But when I imagine myself bringing that book to a room full of people where that one person might be, I wonder if it'll have the reach.*

Neither is wrong. In fact, both have to be faced. For now, it's enough to name what you have access to—what is keeping you here, doing the work that will eventually change someone's life.

Looking back on those 3 years, how have you used the book to get to that place? Who are you working with and how did the book connect you with them?

_____

_____

_____

_____

_____

_____

_____

_____

What happened in the first year after launch that set you on that path?

_____

_____

_____

_____

_____

_____

_____

_____

_____

_____

What's more prominent when you envision "wild success" in your future—you as author, or you in another aspect of life? Does being an author feed into your broader work or does your work support your primary identity as an author?

MAKE
CONNECTIONS

REFINE YOUR UNDERSTANDING OF YOUR OWN *AUTHOR*-ITY, YOUR SPECIFIC READER & THE HEART OF YOUR IDEA

YOUR *AUTHOR*-ITY

SOMETIMES, NOT BEING SPECIAL IS EXACTLY WHAT MAKES US SPECIAL

What does it mean to be an author, really? Take a second with that. Has your definition changed over time? I told you I'd hit you with the existential crises, and I meant it—what does it mean to *be* an author? I've seen us collectively define it has someone whose profession is to write books, but then there are authors of all kinds of publications that earn their living from writing. I've bristled at "writers write," because when do you shift from writer to author, and are you still an author if you're not currently writing? Is it about having a book or making one? Do you have to be published by someone, published somewhere, publish ever?

I'm not sure where you stand right now. It may still be a stretch to consider yourself an author, or you may feel comfortable with the term as long as it's clear you're not putting yourself up next to "the greats" (whomever those are to you). Or maybe you totally own it, no matter how many books are under your belt. My point here is to call attention to the relativity of it all.

"EVERY TIME IT'S TOLD, SOMEONE MAKES $1 MILLION. YOU'RE WELCOME TO DO IT."

—VONNEGUT, ON THE CINDERELLA STORY

Because if authorship is relative, and very probably includes you, as you are, right in this moment, it's also true that your favorite authors—the ones who blew your mind wide open—are in the same exact boat. In my view, you don't get to be *more* author or *less* author any more than you can be more or less human. It's a state of being undefined by productivity or success. It has to be. No one bestows the title upon you like an identity promotion. You simply decide whether to be one, for a season or for a lifetime.

Take a second with that, too. Because this next exercise is about seeing yourself as an author, amongst the authors you love and hate. And it's a seriously important step to take. When you see other authors as folks who are starting conversations similar to or different from the conversation you want to have, they become inspiration and potential collaborators rather than idols, threats, or competition. You realize we're all just operating from our own authority. And you start to seize your own.

How do you imagine readers recommending your book to others?
Start with one sentence you might overhear at a cocktail party.

_____

_____

_____

_____

_____

_____

_____

_____

Who are they recommending it to? A peer, colleague, boss, close
friend? What other books or authors might they compare it to?

_____

_____

_____

_____

_____

_____

_____

_____

_____

List some authors you like and why:

_____

_____

_____

_____

_____

_____

_____

_____

List some authors you don't like and why:

_____

_____

_____

_____

_____

_____

_____

What kind of author do you want to be seen as?

_____

_____

_____

_____

_____

_____

Note: I'm including writing prompts in some sections for anyone with a daily writing practice that they don't want to derail during discovery, for anyone publishing content around their writing process, or for anyone who simply thinks better via writing. If that doesn't resonate with your process, feel free to stash them for later or disregard completely.

EXPLORATION PROMPTS:

Write or record a piece of content around "why I want to write this book." Feel free to be completely self-focused here if needed—you can choose whether or not to publish this. Just give yourself freedom to say it all out loud.

Reflect on why you're going through this effort, from an outcome standpoint. How integral is a book to what you want, personally and professionally? How much are you going to actively leverage it in your envisioned future? Is it going to lead to an ROI worth investing in, or is this a passion project exploration?

Extended prompt: write multiple pieces like this, with the emphasis shifted in each.

Why *I want to write this book*

Why **I** *want to write this book*

Why I **want** *to write this book*

Why I want **to write** *this book*

Why I want to write **this book**

YOUR READER

WRITING IS COMMUNICATION, AND COMMUNICATION IS AN EXCHANGE

I'm a huge fan of writing by comparison. Scaffolding exercises (where you mimic the structure and tone of a poem to write something new) unlocked something in me back before I admitted I was a writer, and the school of thought I was trained under via Story Grid is based on finding and learning from the shapes of stories. This is where I latched on to the Vonnegut "story shapes" speech quoted in the last section, and scaffolding is how I like to break out of blocks to this day.

And also (yes, this is a silly phrase I'm entirely stuck on for emphasis lately—one day you'll be able to date my works by the phrases that are looping in my head)...

The benefit of these exercises can be lost if you forget to tap back into your connection to your reader before it's done. Ask me and my overly complicated and needlessly academic drafts how we know. After naming who you are to your project and how you'd like to step into the world with your book in hand, it's just as important to name who you're handing it to and how they'll show up to that exchange.

YOU DON'T WANT TO CHANGE THE WORLD, YOU JUST WANT TO CHANGE THEIR MINDS. (OR VICE VERSA.)

Notice that I put author and reader identities on equal footing. The nonfiction world is all about their target readers. The closer you are to marketing, the harder it is to step into a project without naming some kind of reader. And yet (there's another go-to phrase of mine)—the audience only matters so far as you're planning to communicate with them. The conversation is what matters.

By this, I mean it's fine to say you want to reach CEOs, but what are CEOs looking for? What are they reading? Are they reading? Are they reading the kind of material you like to write? It's excellent to say you want to reach women, but do you have a specific woman in mind? Have you had this kind of conversation with her before?

This is all doubly true if you're in the "I just want to reach one person" or "my book is for everyone" camp. (Yes, it's one camp— they share a mess hall full of half-finished drafts.) Once you've acknowledged your authorship and authority, there's nothing left to prove about yourself on the page. You're free to communicate your thoughts. So. Who's on the other end of the line?

First, before trying to name who your reader is, tap back into your idea. What will be better for your reader because they read your book?

_____

_____

_____

_____

_____

_____

_____

Is there any kind of caution that comes with that benefit?

_____

_____

_____

_____

_____

_____

_____

_____

If they never, ever get access to your book, what will life be like for them?

_____

_____

_____

_____

_____

Who would most be interested in this improvement, in spite of the caution, because of how much they're feeling that pain without having your book?

_____

_____

_____

_____

_____

_____

What kind of reader is this person? i.e. are they reading for luxury or skimming for takeaways? Are they digging for deep personal change already or are they just here for the tactical?

_____

_____

_____

_____

_____

_____

Who else is writing to this person?

_____

_____

_____

_____

_____

_____

What is their pain point or problem space, having not read your book?

_____

_____

_____

_____

_____

_____

Where have other sources gotten it right, and where have they gotten it wrong?

_____

_____

_____

_____

_____

_____

What does this reader say they want? What do they think will solve their pain point or curiosity?

_____

_____

_____

_____

_____

_____

Do you already have clientele or other interactions with your target or secondary audience? What kind of avatar or demographic profile do you have for them?

_____

_____

_____

_____

_____

_____

Can you attach this reader to a real life human that you know? (A younger-version-of-you counts!)

_____

_____

_____

_____

_____

_____

Have you brought this topic to their attention before, directly or indirectly? What was helpful, what was not?

_____

_____

_____

_____

_____

_____

EXPLORATION PROMPTS:

Write or record 2-3 pieces of content dedicated to these specific individuals, real or imagined.

Let them know you see them and their struggle.

YOUR IDEA

BIG IDEAS DON'T START THAT WAY—THEY GROW BY INVITING PEOPLE IN

You might have figured out by now that I'm not going to sign off on your idea as "good enough." Personally, I'd be suspicious of anyone who said just that. The way that question is usually phrased to me is, "Do I have a book here?" And the answer is entirely up to you. The answer is *always* up to you. Anything can be spun. Anything can be worked into a book, a film, a poem, a painting. The deciding factor is the individual author's vision and patience. Whether or not it's "good" is up to the individual reader's preference.

So when nonfiction is considered "Big Idea" I want you to know that it's just as relative as *good idea* or *am I an author*. There is no measuring contest that can tell you that you've won biggest idea. My admonition/encouragement from the authority conversation applies here too: comparison is not the same as competition. As you're working through this section and the next (and the rest of your project...and life), look at what comes up for what it is and nothing more.

"NO ARMY CAN WITHSTAND... AN IDEA WHOSE TIME HAS COME."
—VICTOR HUGO, SO GOODREADS TELLS ME

By that, I mean our impulse to find a salacious, exciting, juicy, or intriguing topic that's "exciting enough" is less about what the book actually needs and more about what we think might compensate for whatever still has us feeling unsure of our *authority*.

Better questions:

- Is my idea *connected* enough to a real reader?
- Is my book *authentic enough* to my views and experience?
- Is my story *present enough* to build trust?

Since even these questions will trip us up in imposter-land, I prefer to stay in the vein of the last set of questions we answered. You already validated (or are in the process of validating) the presence of a need to be met. You know who is feeling that need and what they're looking for. You're ready to meet them there. If you want your idea to be *Big*—if you want to make a real difference with it—start there and then go deeper. Invite them to a deeper truth. Even the smallest ideas grow to a phenomena, not by being the most dramatic, but by inviting others to latch on. To join the conversation.

Even if someone promised your reader a path to what they want, what do you know they actually need?

_____

_____

_____

_____

_____

_____

_____

What would change for them if they could access this need?

_____

_____

_____

_____

_____

_____

_____

_____

Because of your expertise, experience, or analysis, you probably also know that they won't be able to meet that need until something more happens. There's a truth that they're currently missing, a deeper realization they need to uncover. What is that truth?

_____

_____

_____

_____

_____

_____

_____

_____

WORKING SUMMARY MADLIB:

My reader is looking for my book because they want _____, and I can help them with that through _____. But unless they can access _____, they're always going to come up short. That's why _____ has always failed them before. So we're also going to work on _____, which will give them _____. I know this will work because _____, and I can't wait to see the shift in them, just as I've seen _____.

NOTES:

_____
_____
_____
_____
_____
_____
_____
_____
_____
_____
_____
_____
_____
_____
_____
_____
_____
_____
_____
_____
_____
_____
_____
_____
_____
_____

SEE WHAT
COMES UP

REIMAGINE YOUR NEXT STEPS:

5 – 4 – 3 – 2 – 1, TABLE OF CONTENT & DIVING IN

5 - 4 - 3 - 2 - 1

CONSTRAINTS KEEP YOU PRESENT & PRESENCE IS FLOW

There are a number of reasons I prefer to write nonfiction over fiction, and at the top of the list is just how many possibilities there are to choose from. In fiction, I mean. The sheer realm of potential freaks me *out*. The tradeoff, of course, is that nonfiction is closer to the overt truth, which can create the opposite experience. What do you do when it all hits too close to home and there's no fairy godmother to bring in to save the day? You set some enabling constraints.

Trying to solve the whole problem at once is futile and exhausting. And a really good way to never, ever get your work out the door (sneaky, brain. I see you). The tools that follow won't make you turn into a pumpkin at midnight, but they can help you find that sweet spot between too many options and too little breathing room. Keep your focus on one thing at a time, and trust that it's all building toward this project's happily ever after.

WHEN ONE ACCESS POINT IS BLOCKED, ZOOM OUT AND TRY ANOTHER

Quick caveat: Among other experiences and sources, Story Grid concepts factor heavily into this progression. However, these are not Story Grid specific tools, are not associated directly with Story Grid, and do not represent any attempt at teaching Story Grid concepts or any other organization or school of thought. It's just a really cool progression that has helped unlock folks over the years.

- First, run a 5-minute outline to see what's at the surface (or hiding just under the surface) of your ideation. Recordings are available at *brannansirratt.com/five-minute-outline* for a guided experience.
- Next, map out a 4-quadrant progression of your content.
- Now explore the way 3 narrative devices will get you there.
- Finally, reconnect with the 2 POVs that you can access as you're drafting and revising your 1 Big Idea.

What can I learn about my message in a 5 minute, no judgments check-in?

MINUTE ONE: What's the key takeaway—the one thing I need the reader to "get"?

_____
_____
_____
_____
_____
_____
_____
_____

MINUTE TWO: Why do we care about this topic?

_____
_____
_____
_____
_____
_____
_____
_____
_____

MINUTE THREE: What stands in between us and the key take-away? Why do we resist or get stuck?

_____

_____

_____

_____

_____

_____

MINUTE FOUR: What makes us believe the key takeaway is for us? What anchors us to it?

_____

_____

_____

_____

_____

_____

MINUTE FIVE: What's the big invitation for the reader? What's really on the other side of "getting" the takeaway?

_____

_____

_____

_____

_____

_____

After writing freely for each minute, summarize what comes up here in outline form. **Important: notice where each minute goes on the outline.**

2	Minute two—create connection in the setup
3	Minute three—progressively build out the topic
1	*Minute one—name a specific takeaway*
4	Minute four—anchor the reader to the takeaway
5	Minute five—payoff the initial connection with an honest "other side" of the takeaway

Can I see this content structured into a 4-quadrant progression that guides the reader to a new perspective?

1. PROPOSITIONAL TRUTH: What insight, observation, experience, or process am I exploring?

_____

_____

_____

_____

_____

_____

_____

2. PROCEDURAL STEPS: How can my understanding, exploration, or process be broken down into a sequence? (First, next, then...)

_____

_____

_____

_____

_____

_____

_____

_____

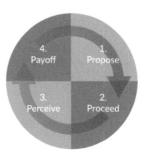

3. PERSPECTIVE SHIFT: What is the deeper shift in thinking that my content asks of the reader or demonstrates via my memoir?

_____

_____

_____

_____

_____

_____

4. PARTICIPATORY PAYOFF: What does integration of my propositional truth really look like?

_____

_____

_____

_____

_____

_____

_____

What roles do the 3 nonfiction narrative devices or genre dimensions (worldview analysis, how-to, narrative journey) play?

What kind of analysis or new understanding needs to be explored for the reader's worldview to change?

_____

_____

_____

_____

_____

_____

_____

What kind of obvious, prescriptive, or tangible outcome needs to be delivered for the reader to know how to bring their new worldview into their day to day life?

_____

_____

_____

_____

_____

_____

_____

What kind of narrative journey needs to be included for the reader to connect with the more challenging aspects of this change?

_____

_____

_____

_____

_____

_____

Which of these do you anticipate writing from the most?

_____

_____

_____

_____

_____

_____

_____

Legend:
- Worldview Analysis
- Tangible How-to
- Narrative Journey

Categories: Setup, Build, Crisis, Anchor, Payoff

How can I draw on the 2 key perspectives of this content (mine and my reader's) as I write?

Me: How can I tap into my process of exploration, tangible experience, or ongoing transformation? When I talk about this topic, is it personal or more general? What's natural to talk about and what's more of a stretch?

_____

_____

_____

_____

_____

_____

My Reader: How can I connect to my reader and a need I'd like to meet for them? Have I already met this need, or am I in search of answers? What's natural to talk about and what's more of a stretch?

_____

_____

_____

_____

_____

_____

With all of this in mind, what's the 1 sentence I can now distill the Big Idea of this book into?

_____

_____

_____

_____

_____

_____

_____

_____

_____

_____

_____

_____

_____

_____

TABLE OF CONTENT

THREE DIMENSIONAL ARCS COME TOGETHER ONE LAYER AT A TIME

The table of contents in a book is one of the last things to be proofed and a very sneaky place for errors to slip through anyway. It's an end stage formatting tool. Some books don't even have it. So why the hell do we think we need an outline that looks like a table of contents from the very beginning of our nonfiction projects?

Caveat, again: Our overarching goal, at any and all times, is for you to *go with whatever you have access to*. If you've got a vision for your chapter progression that feels fantastic, looks exactly like you want it to in the final book (for now) and inspires you to start writing, do the damn thing until you can't. Then come back if you need another access point.

Now. Did I have a sneaky error slip through in this title? Nope. Just a ridiculous pun that has stuck around. While I don't find it necessary or often helpful to create a table of contents before there is content, I do like to make a table in which I plot out said content. That's what we're looking at next.

"ART IS NOT A THING. IT IS A WAY."

—ELBERT HUBBARD, WHO I KNEW NOTHING ABOUT BEFORE THIS QUOTE BUT REALLY SUPER WANT TO LEARN MORE

The thing is, paintings aren't made from left to right or top to bottom, filling inch by inch of the canvas with a perfect slice of the image. They're built from the inside out, layer by abstract layer. The artist's vision keeps them going—whether it's to roll with the inspiration as it comes or to set the tone from the very first strokes. As a not-painter, I have exactly zero clue what's happening in any given moment. It just looks like a mess for a good long while. But that's the expectation, so I trust the process (and marvel as it unfolds).

Whoever set your expectations at "write clean from top to bottom or it doesn't count" needs to come see me. I have an unofficial TED talk I'd like to give them. Because (brace yourselves, all you who're still coping with the "author" identity): you're an artist too. You get to be messy. You get to play with tones and layers and refinement long past what anyone else thinks is done or to stop at a point of abstraction only a certain few will "get." That may take a while to settle into if you're not already there, so for now we're just going to name what some of those layers are. Hang with me. Get messy. Trust the process.

NARRATIVE JOURNEY LAYER

Here, sketch out the **process of transformative change** that your book conveys or asks of the reader. Reference your narrative dimension in #3 in the last section if you need a jumpstart. It can also be helpful to start with a prompt, like a Hero's Journey, Virgin's Promise, or any other universal process of change.

The goal of this layer is to name the steps of change from where you or the reader begin to the place of deeper truth where you or the reader will end. Naming the steps (crossing the threshold, caught shining, etc) is more important here than choosing specific stories...yet. But as always, if you've got access to it, go for it!

We're attaching deep change to a narrative journey because we do not like change, generally speaking, and do much better *watching* it happen than being told to do it ourselves. So when you attach the deepest parts of the work to real stories, the reader gets to relax into those emotions without being expressly asked to deal with their own. The stories can come from you personally, a specific case study, or collections of stories, but they should be told narratively and they should attach to a clear progression of change.

Important: Yes, you can work these layers out in any order, but when you're on a specific layer it's important right now to *stay* *with that layer.* Don't think about whether this step 6 aligns with the others. That's when we start to shoehorn content around and everything gets performative and weird.

We're going full *Shrek* with these layers, baby. Save the pretty parfait for later. They are onions and proud of it.

UNIVERSAL PROCESS STEPS	STORY THAT STEP MIGHT ATTACH TO
e.g. The Ordinary World	*e.g. I Thought I Knew Everything*
The Hero Returned	I Didn't Know Shit (But I Learned It!)

WORLDVIEW ANALYSIS LAYER

For this list, the work is to figure out **how the reader sees the world** (or how you did, if you're closer to memoir) at the beginning of the book, how they'll see it differently at the end of the book, and what moves them along that journey.

Note: This layer is called "academic" in a lot of my material and Story Grid's material, which can be a bit of a misnomer or deterrent. Here's the thing—**not all analysis is academia**, but there are some seriously good things we can learn from that space. Like creating a little bit of distance so that it's safe to really pick something apart without feeling attacked, or leading with genuine curiosity and willingness to learn, experiment, and be wrong. I'd love to geek out more about that with you, but for now swap it out for "analysis" only and it gets you to the heart of the task.

To wrap your head around this list (and the corresponding analysis layer you named in #3 above), try taking the word "world-view" really literally: if your reader is sitting at home, holding your book for whatever reason, what is their view of the world in that moment? Going back to **your specific reader** workshopping will help here, with their pain points and what they say they want.

I like to picture an old pixellated video game—the kind where you can't see the whole map until you move around a bit. The first steps in this list are you letting them know you see where they are on the map and telling them where you are (your world-view). Then you can **progressively bring light** to the places on the map between the two of you until there is a clear path they can follow.

HOW THE WORLDVIEW IS CHANGING	WHAT THE READER NEEDS TO KNOW FOR THAT CHANGE TO BE POSSIBLE
e.g. Blissfully ignorant to aware	*e.g. New Data Says "Look Out!"*
Brand New Perspective	The View Is Better from This Angle

This is another layer/list that is named differently on some of my other worksheets and articles: in those spaces, it's called "how-to." Like the academic analysis dilemma, this can be a distraction if you're not already writing a how-to. But if you've got a takeaway, you need a how-to layer—if nothing else to tell them how-to-take-away the takeaway.

What I really love about this layer is how it can shift their attention from want to need. Your reader is here for a reason, and that reason is primarily selfish. That's not a judgment, just the truth of how we spend our time. They want something. How you decide to deliver it is up to you, but the promise of that thing is going to keep them turning the pages.

So your "how-to" doesn't necessarily have to tell anyone how to do anything. You don't have to have a process or a set of steps or a listicle here. You just need something they can grab onto and say that they "got it" and can take with them after the book is back on the shelf.

Clear as mud? Here's an example:

My reader is here for me to help them get their book planned out. I know they need to tap into their own authorial sense of agency. I'm going to step them through the process of naming all the important parts of their book, but also step them through the process of naming all the important parts of themselves as a creator. At the end, they could have a book plan if they're still interested (and still have a book in them), but they won't feel as attached to my approval of it. (See what I did there?)

WHAT THE READER WANTS	WHAT YOU KNOW THEY NEED
e.g. Magic Pill, Please	*e.g. Someone to trust*
To keep engaging with you, because you're honest	A glass of water for that bitter magic pill

TOP-LAYER TOPIC SYNTHESIS (OR: TAKE A STAB AT AN OUTLINE)

You might start here if you already have an outline, or play here until multiple iterations finally lock into one that feels good to write from. Or you might skip it all together. Sometimes it takes me a really long time to get to a "proper" outline for myself or a client, because there's more that I need to uncover before the specific chapters feel clear.

Some things to keep in mind as you get closer and closer to a map of your draft or revision:

- Try to think of each line as a topic bucket rather than a chapter. If I had a dollar for every minute I've spent staring at an unfinished chapter, only to realize it was a complete idea that just needed to blend into another chapter...Don't paint yourself into a corner.
- There are certain phrases in the writing community, like "page one rewrite" and "starting over from scratch" and "rewriting the whole thing" and "please God can we be done" that I wish we could eliminate. Try to think of your outlines as a hypothesis, and drafting as an experiment. If what you map out doesn't work and needs to be retooled, you haven't lost anything. Not time or effort or words. You've only gained data/inputs/ideas. It's good work. Keep it up.
- Remember, there are a thousand iterations of your book that are "right." We're just looking for the one that feels

accessible to you and your reader right now. Save the outlines and ideas that feel good but not right. Who knows what they might become later.

Your play space starts here...

So when are the three separate layers (top-level doesn't matter so much here...not yet) "done" and ready to move into the table? You can probably already see that putting it all side by side could get complicated fast—so don't start here unless you're really good at holding your focus to one thing at a time.

If you're like me and cannot, then play with each list separately until it looks like a decently logical progression from point "hm this book looks interesting" to point "woah, I (see the world/ myself/my want) differently now!"

By logical, I mean you're setting the reader up as Kurt Vonnegut's Man in a Hole plot. And if you haven't seen that yet, drop everything and go to brannansirratt.com and scroll down till you see his name. Click. Watch. Enjoy. Come back.

Ready? Ok, so you're meeting the reader wherever they are—probably "mostly fine, but curious about how things could be better"—then dropping the bottom out from under them with whatever curiosity or problem or pain you're digging into.

That'll happen somewhere in the first few chapters: your *proposition* space. You propose that the world could actually be significantly better, because look at how hard it really is.

After that, you've got to build them a ladder and help them climb out of it. That happens step by step (*procedurally*, if you will), and too big a leap may mean they can't stay with you to get out of the hole.

Then, just as their head pops out to blue skies above ground, you help them see how much their *perspective* has shifted after all that undergroundedness, and they've got to reckon with real change they hadn't quite expected. If you don't prepare them for that or meet them there in that discomfort, you may lose them altogether.

If you don't lose them, if you're able to move them along with you beat for beat of this journey to a new way of thinking or doing or being in the world, then they get the option to *participate* with you in that way of thinking. And if you're really honest with them, (and you should be) that won't be all blue skies either. But it'll be worth it. And you'll tell them why.

You can see how each point of that process is about keeping the reader with you. It's not "drop man into a hole and leave him there." The arc has to come back up. So making sure your lists make decently logical sense in terms of what it's asking of the reader, what you'll need to give them along the way, and how far you can realistically take them...that's what "done" looks like here.

When you have that for all three arcs, plug them in, as they are, again without any judgment or panic. Then your table becomes the hypothesis, and the chapter maps become the experimentation space. Pull the text out from the table to the map. Run a 5 minute outline for just that chapter. See if *that one row* makes sense. If not, play around with what would make *that 5 minute outline* make sense. See what we're doing here? One focus at at time, one solution at at time, one experiment at a time. It's all good data. And hey, if at any point you get the itch to just write, step. away. from the spreadsheet. Go write. You've been unlocked. Come back if you get stuck.

CHAPTERS	TRANSFORMATIVE JOURNEY LAYER	WORLDVIEW ANALYSIS LAYER	TANGIBLE OUTCOME LAYER
Introduce your proposition			
Make a case for the proposition			
Anchor the proposition to reality or need			
Build the idea procedurally			
Build the idea procedurally			
Build the idea procedurally			
Shift the lens to deeper topics			
Intro the perspective shift			
Build the perspective shift			
Anchor the perspective shift			
Invite participation			
Name honest outcomes			
Proposition comes full circle			

CHAPTER 1

Transformative Journey:
Worldview Analysis:
Tangible Outcome:
Reader wants:
But needs:

O U T L I N E :

1. *Hook/Why we care*
2. *Topics/What's in our way*
3. *Takeaway*
4. *Anchor/Why we'll believe*
5. *Payoff/What's the invitation*

TOTALLY RIDICULOUS EXAMPLE

Transformative Journey: Caught Shining / the Fairy Godmother Story
Worldview Analysis: What makes fairy godmothers pick someone to help
Tangible Outcome: Hope that anyone can be helped
Reader wants: To go to the ball like I did
But needs: To see herself as worthy of the ball

OUTLINE:

1. *Hook/Why we care:* Fairy Godmother found me and saw something in me and dressed me up and sent me off
2. *Topics/What's in our way:* Why would she do that? What's a fairy godmother's M.O. anyway? Why would she do that for me?
3. *Takeaway:* My invitation has always been waiting—so has yours
4. *Anchor/Why we'll believe:* Empathy - I need to get more vulnerable here. Probably go deeper into what I was thinking when she first appeared.
5. *Payoff/What's the invitation:* It wasn't what she gave me, it was how she helped me see myself differently—the way she sees us all.

DIVING IN

GIVE YOUR EDITOR BRAIN
A LOLLIPOP SO YOUR CREATIVE
BRAIN CAN SHINE

We've spent so much time on structural pieces and naming and mapping and plotting that it could be really easy to spin yourself into oblivion and never come back. I don't mean come back to *me*, either. This is written as a summary of my process and will be more effective in partnership, yes. But my genuine interest is in seeing you unlock your ideas. I mean it's easy to spin yourself away from your *writing*.

If ten other famous authors have talked about your topic... if you don't have the tenure or time that others have...if you don't get the story down *just right*...if if if. There will always be a reason to keep planning and never write *if you want to look for that reason.* So the last thing I want is for you to feel like this booklet and process is a required step, from start to finish, before you can write a word. Nope. We're unlocking doors here. As soon as you've got a way in, take it. Tell your editor brain to trust that what you've validated so far will serve you later. Then go experiment. Not finding that door? Here are a few you might try.

YOU'RE NOT BLOCKED OR LAZY. YOU'RE AT A LOCKED DOOR. LET'S GET A KEY.

- Do you have a really clear takeaway for the book? If not, it'll be hard to attach it to anything without meandering. Try pulling back to name it clearly OR just let yourself free write for a while to see what comes up.
- Do you have a really clear audience? Does it need to be refined?
- Are you showing up as your most authentic self? Are you posturing or hiding in a way that might hold you back?
- Do you need to create some added layers of safety?
- Do you speak more freely than you write? Consider talking out your work with a friend or colleague, then mocking up outlines and notes from that conversation (or transcript). Writing can be just as effective when jotting down ideas here and there as it is when you're sitting down to work-work.

- Do you have a "masterwork" or comp to refer to? Try some scaffolding exercises from your favorite author's outline or introduction. Try some from an author you don't love. See what the new perspective opens up for you.

- Finish this sentence: When I talk to someone about this topic, I find that I often...

- Create this reminder for yourself, then refer to it when you're feeling stuck: When I am flowing on this topic, I am often driven by...
  - Curiosity, always asking more questions and digging for more answers
  - Expertise, confident about sharing something that you know will help someone
  - Experience, passionate about relaying wins and cautions that will build the reader up
  - Hope, cautiously optimistic about what doors a shift in perspective, change in behavior, and greater awareness could open for the reader

- Don't forget you can jump in and out and around your project—paintings don't happen from one side of the canvas to the other. If one section feels blocked, check your table and try another.

- Do you have too many answers in your book? Have you created a scenario for yourself where you have to be the expert when really you just want to explore? Check your outline for areas where it feels unnecessarily restrictive or strict.

- Do you have too few answers, when you know you actually could be more direct?
- Try writing the section you're interested in (but stuck on) in a different style or genre. Get more prescriptive. Get more narrative. Be a scientist. Be a sci-fi novelist. Be a poet. Step outside of your plan for just a minute, get some fresh perspective, and see what comes up.

NOTES:

_____

_____

_____

_____

_____

_____

_____

_____

_____

_____

_____

_____

_____

_____

THE POWER OF YOU

STORY IS IN OUR BONES— HAVE YOU MADE IT TO THE MARROW?

I'm not sure I can squeeze one more metaphor into this book, but if that's what it will take to see your eyes light up and your idea lock into place, get on my calendar. I'll give you *all the metaphors*. Because that's the point of everything.

Not just my work or your work or who gets what book published where. It's the point of *everything*. We are here to make meaning in this life, and if you've made enough meaning that you feel even the slightest inclination to share it, then let's do whatever it takes to make that thing happen.

So yes. Story is in your blood and your bones and your guts and it's so incredibly weird to lay your guts out on the table for strangers to dissect—but who ever said being a human was anything but weird?

And yeah, you're playing a video game with your readers and giving them a map they can follow (and tools to take on their quest). And the process is a stinky ogre onion. And there are charts and layers and quadrants and arrows.

NOW YOU KNOW THAT IT'S HERE, YOU CAN GET BACK WHENEVER YOU WANT.

And you and your story and the wisdom inside of it are the ocean itself. Even if you just stay on the shoreline of that idea, there's enough power there to move the earth itself. You didn't come to that idea by accident, and you can't be passive about it now that you're here.

You can choose a lot of things—to just sit down and look at it for a while. To look for a few seashells—a blog post here, a side project there. To play a game with some friends. To dive in deep. To build a house. You can choose a lot of things, including walking away and living that landlocked life for a while. But you'll always know it's here. You'll always know how to get back if you ever change your mind.

You didn't get here by accident. You've earned it along every step of your journey from birth to now. If you want to document this moment in time, this journey so far, this wisdom you have right now—maybe it's time to wade in.

I hope this process has helped. I hope you know how power-ful you are. I hope you feel that power every step of the way. See you on the shore.

RESOURCES

- Kurt Vonnegut's "Shapes of Story" presentation is an epic reminder that templates work and mimicry is a natural part of art. I love the Man in a Hole plot for most nonfiction.
- Nancy Duarte's "Secret Structure of Great Talks" TED talk is an incredible visualization of powerful communication (and writing is just good communication.)
- Story Grid's Big Idea Nonfiction conference blew my mind wide open. You can do the full deep dive course (beware the rip current—or at least be prepared to body surf it), and you can check out the articles it inspired for me after I got back. They are:
  - Narrative Device: On the Origin of Story
  - Nonfiction Storytelling Commandments
  - Unlock Your Nonfiction Book
  - The 5 Minute Chapter Outline
  - Nonfiction and Fiction Genre Dimensions

- The 5 Minute Outline is expanded on my site to include recordings and some context to help you use it. brannansirratt.com/five-minute-outline

Clients who engage at a discovery level or higher have access to a living resource database filled with recordings, teaching sessions, and handouts that support our work together. Folks who purchase just the resource database also get access to a discovery call. In other words, I don't want you to leave a call empty handed or juggle info without a call to support you.

Writing is hard. No matter what we do to create flow, make it clearer, or release judgment, it's not easy to tap into something that's inside of you and package it up for someone else to take with them.

Writing is good and natural and fun and beautiful...and hard. You shouldn't have to do it alone.

ABOUT THE AUTHOR

Brannan Sirratt is a long-time ghostwriter, line editor, and developmental coach who is constantly working to up-level her understanding of story. With a primary focus on nonfiction, Brannan believes that story is the quickest and arguably only way that we experience and convey change, making it the most valuable tool in anyone's arsenal—regardless of genre. She has a passion for helping authors who have something big to say but feel tangled up in the nuance of writing, which has led to the Reluctant Drafter project, the 5 Minute Outline process, and both 1:1 and group client work focused on getting (and keeping) folks writing. *brannansirratt.com* for support, resources, and consults.

Made in the USA
Monee, IL
14 April 2023

31308172R00057